THE DITTY BAG BOOK

A Guide for Sailors

Frank Rosenow
illustrated by the author

Skyhorse Publishing

Skyhorse Publishing books may be purchased in bulk at special discounts for sales promotion, corporate gifts, fund-raising, or educational purposes. Special editions can also be created to specifications. For details, contact the Special Sales Department, Skyhorse Publishing, 307 West 36th Street, 11th Floor, New York, NY 10018 or info@skyhorsepublishing.com.

www.skyhorsepublishing.com

10 9 8 7 6 5 4 3 2 1

Library of Congress Cataloging-in-Publication Data

Rosenow, Frank, 1944-
  The ditty bag book : a guide for sailors / by Frank Rosenow.
    p. cm.
  ISBN 978-1-61608-187-4 (pbk. : alk. paper)
  1. Sails--Maintenance and repair. 2. Masts and rigging--Maintenance and repair. 3. Ditty bags. I. Title.
  VM531.R67 2011
  623.8'62--dc22

                                          2010039699

Printed in China

Cover Note

Before the advent of steam, the hand-seaming palm was the most jealously guarded item in the personal ditty bag of every conscientious sailor. Sailors and sailmakers who took pride in their work often made up their own palms, fitting an indented iron to a leather sling made to fit their working hand exactly. The raised metal piece was used, of course, to brace against the head of a threaded needle and push it effortlessly through canvas. These seaming palms were sometimes improved with the addition of a metal or leather "thumb stall" ferrule that you could slip over the thumb so that a turn of twine could be wound up on it to heave tight after a stitch.

The palm on the cover, which I've sketched against the backdrop of a rudimentary ditty bag to which a brass lanyard ring is being stitched, is superior to a plain seaming palm in that it *incorporates* a protruding leather thumb-guard round which twine can be taken to heave home. This type of palm was originally developed for heavy-duty seaming, such as bolt rope stitching to a sail, and hence is known as a "roping palm." But today it is used for all kinds of hand seaming by professionals, and represents the finest possible acquisition for the recreational sailor's ditty bag.

—F. R.

THE TOOLS

THE PROCESSES

1.

The Tools

Few things on board a boat afford its owner or crew as much satisfaction as keeping a trim craft in rope, rigging, and sails. To achieve this, the sailor of yore carried a cotton duck ditty bag with a carefully selected assortment of tools that enabled him, in substantial measure, to render the same services to his vessel as a full-blown sailmaker or rigger. The contents of the ditty bag also served as a darning kit for his wardrobe, and as a source of materials for practicing decorative knotting and other seafaring arts.

As such objectives are as legitimate and necessary on the cruising or racing sailboat of today, or can be undertaken for the sheer pleasure of it in some land-bound nook, I will here make an inventory of the traditional tools—with some additions prompted by technological advances and the reign of synthetic materials—that you will find of use in all manner of canvas (including Dacron and nylon) and rope work on board.

The Sailmaker's Bench

There is no denying that the ditty bag concept owes its tools and methodology in large measure to professional sailmakers and, to a lesser extent, riggers. Let us therefore begin with a passing glance at a right-handed sailanaker's bench and see how it is professionally utilized, even though it is unlikely that this particular tool will fit into your fo'c's'le, let alone the ditty bag.

The right-handed sailmaker's bench shown in **Fig. 1** (for a left-hander, the bench ends and work direction would have to be mirrored) is designed mainly for hand seaming, but since its occupant has a wide selection of tools within easy reach, the wooden bench can be adapted to every phase of traditional sailmaking—except panel cutting, which is most conveniently done on the floor. Benches employed in land-locked lofts are recognized by their straight legs, while a sea-going bench spreads its legs wide for stability as befits a nautical character.

The most comfortable height of the bench or the more compact sewing stool (an alternative for on-board use if fitted with an attachment point for a sailhook lanyard, a couple of holes for fids, and a shelf or canvas bag for oddments) of

Fig. 1

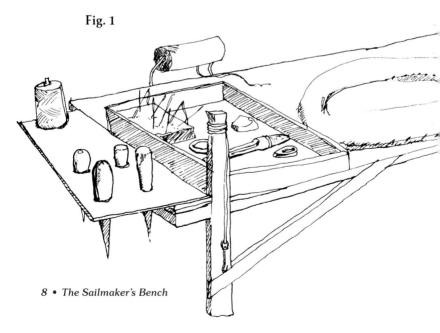

course will depend on the length of your own legs. I am six feet tall with legs to match and work comfortably on the 15"-high bench in the drawing. This may seem low, but there is a reason for it, as we shall see.

But try it out for yourself. You're sitting on a cushion which can slide along the 6'-long bench. On your right, there's a small, holed shelf to hold the fid collection, and a pin around which the roll of seaming twine can revolve. Nestled in just beside you to the right is a 10" × 16" area bordered by a 1" rim. In this cozy nook, which was referred to as the "cow pasture" when I was apprenticed, you can leave your palm and needles (stuck into a soft felt pad where they are readily at hand), along with clew rings, beeswax, knife, thimbles, and the half-dozen other items you'll want within arm's reach. At the far outside corner, the pasture is overlooked by a 20"-high post (actually an extension of one leg) which has a sail-hook and lanyard twisted round the top. Some benches, notably in the U.S., lack this post, the sailmaker simply looping the lanyard through a hole, instead.

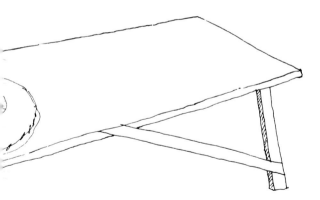

Our man on the job in **Fig. 2** demonstrates the hook's use. He is in the process of flat-seaming, joining two cloth panels which he has tucked in and overlapped at the edge to prevent fraying. The sailmaker's hook is inserted at the seam, enabling him to tension the cloth with his left hand while taking stitches with his right. The lower cloth is doubled back so that left-handed tension can be applied near to where the stitches are being taken.

The workpiece is draped over his knees and, when positioned correctly, his upper body is nearly at a right angle to the seam, with stitches being taken in the vicinity of his right thigh. This is the reason for the low bench—it elevates the knee to a position where a workpiece resting on it is within comfortable reach.

If you look closely, you may also be able to see that our sailmaker is using a roping palm. To heave home a stitch properly, he has let the needle slip out of the iron and under his ring finger, so that he can take a turn of twine around the thumb guard and pull tight on the stitch.

As the seam progresses, he'll slide down along the bench on his cushion, unlaying the sailhook lanyard from the post from time to time to reinsert the hook closer to where he is stitching, thus lending stability to the work.

Fig. 2

A sailmaker's or bosun's principal rope and canvas tool—a stubby, broad-bladed knife—would be carried strapped to his back, where he could reach it with either hand when aloft. More often than not it was homemade. I recall, for instance, a fine-looking Norwegian sailor's knife which bears the inscription: "Laget av seilmaker Halvorsen av en saks i Australia 1900." ("Fashioned in 1900 from a pair of Australian scissors by sailmaker Halvorsen.")

However, for the purpose of this sample inventory of a functional, present-day ditty bag, I prefer to break with such homespun tradition and introduce a smaller, more versatile type of knife.

For the first and foremost ditty bag tool, then, look for a handy clasp knife with a non-corroding blade. I use one with a 3" blade (**Fig. 3**) made of hardened Swedish cutting-edge steel which reaches excellent sharpness. A larger variety (**Fig. 4**) might have a 4" blade, a catch to lock the blade in exposed position, and a hole for fitting a lanyard, and thus be more suitable for general use above and beyond ditty bag chores. All you really need for canvas and rope work, though, is one high-quality blade and a comfortable handle in wood or plastic.

Fig. 3

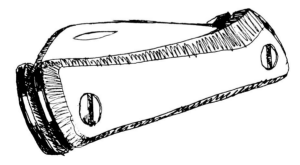

A sharp, thin blade will make it a simple matter to cut sailcloth along warp or fill, or even on the bias if you have a penciled guideline. When cutting canvas (or, of course, its synthetic counterpart), spread the workpiece flat on a floor or clear deck space, tensioning the section to be cut with your left hand and/or knees and elbows. Do not cut from the top downward, but rather from *under* the canvas, with the knife blade pointed up.

There are those who use scissors in canvas work, but there is little a really sharp knife can't do as well, and with greater versatility.

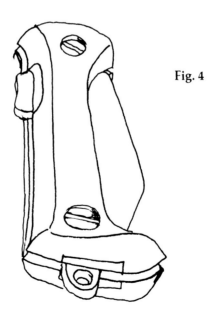

Fig. 4

Sharpening Stone

Sharpening stones come in diverse materials, sizes, and shapes. Today, the most common variety is a man-made synthetic, usually Carborundum. Many of these stones feature a rough side and a smooth side, so that they can first be used to "rough-sharpen" a dull edge, then turned over and applied to the task of really producing a fine, relatively burr-free edge.

The edge thus achieved satisfies most needs, but for the stickler who wants to go all the way, there is soft and hard Arkansas oilstone, quarried from novaculite deposits near Hot Springs. These super-smooth stones are a delight to handle, and with a final burnish on the hard stone's jet-black surface deliver the finest edge possible (short of leather strapping in the old barbershop style). But for the general purposes of the ditty bag, keeping a stone handy so that you can give the blade of your knife a quick honing from dull to sharp whenever you feel it lacks bite, I would settle for a two-sided Carborundum stone measuring at least $1\frac{1}{2}'' \times 3''$—and preferably a bit more. Novaculite is mainly for "finishing" an already sharp surface.

To sharpen a knife, hold the blade parallel to one end of the stone and "slice" across the length of the stone, applying firm but not forced downward pressure from the heel of the blade to the tip. Do this in only one direction, away from the body for one side of the blade, and toward the body for the other side. The blade should be kept at about a 20° angle to the stone (**Fig. 5**). The knife should be turned over on alternate strokes or at short intervals so that the blade is sharpened equally on both sides.

The chore is made easier by a few drops of lubricant on the surface of the stone, either light, sewing machine type oil or just plain water. If the pores of the stone still become clogged with fine grit and/or dried oil residue, give it a thorough wash-out with gasoline.

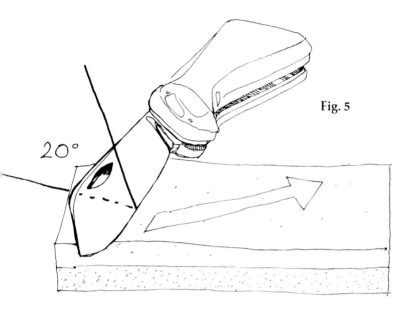

20°

Fig. 5

Seaming Implements   Needles

Sailmaker's needles for a variety of canvas work come in sizes
from #4 (extra large) to #18 (extra small), in accordance
with Standard Wire Gauge classification—the number relat-
ing to the thickness of the round part of the needle. Needle-
making is a British tradition, and the finest of them still origi-
nate from England. I find a #12 useful for guiding the line in
fancy fishline knotting, but for regular seaming and rope
work on a sailboat, only sizes from #14½ through #18 will
have to be considered.

A #14½ needle (this is the sole half-size in the series) is appropriate for sewn rings and other heavy-duty seaming, such as sewing a bolt rope to sails. A #15 functions well in corner stitching through several layers of cloth, and a #16 for stitching together two medium-weight cloth pieces. For light Dacron or duck, a #17 might be best, while nylon spinnaker cloth usually warrants nothing larger than a #18. But doubtlessly you'll form your own preferences as you go along.

A pointed, triangular section is invariably found in the cutting portion of the needle. There are two variations on this characteristic. The "Short Square" or "Lolley" (after English needlesmith William Lolley) is designed for use with round, firm-lay twine and consequently has a rather pronounced eye and a comparatively large cutting triangle to create enough of an opening for the threaded eye to pass through without difficulty (**Fig. 6**). This needle is often selected for decorative stitching, which firm twine makes more distinctive.

"Long Square" needles have a finer taper or "reduced edge" in the cutting section and feature an extended shank that ends in a well integrated eye (**Fig. 7**). This type of needle is excellent for pre-waxed or other flat or soft-lay twine, which pulls down neatly around the eye and does not require a hole much larger than the diameter of the shank to pass through.

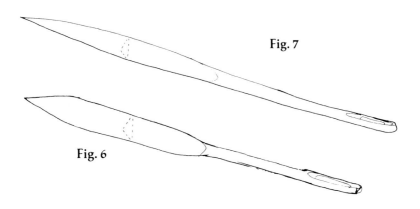

Fig. 7

Fig. 6

For general seaming work, to my mind the best combination is a reduced-edge needle with soft or flat twine which flows through the canvas with a minimum of resistance. I also prefer the Long Square from the point of view that the long shank seems to further a quick, accurate aim when spacing the stitching.

Needles are usually distributed in lots of 25 wrapped up in brown paper envelopes (**Fig. 8**) with an inner wax paper lining to prevent moisture from entering. Needle rust is a problem, especially on shipboard. The needles are made of polished, cast steel and moisture affects them almost immediately. If you allow any surface blemish to develop, the needle will of course become more difficult to sew with, on account of the increased friction. Another storage problem is that the fine points of the needles are easily blunted if knocked around.

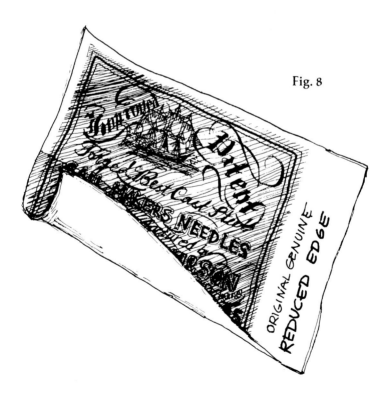

Fig. 8

The sailor of old usually kept his needle-collection in a horn or tube filled with evil-smelling tallow. I would rather recommend smearing an empty tobacco box (**Fig. 9**) or some-such tin container with Vaseline and dropping in the needles with an extra, individual dab of the stuff. The Vaseline both prevents the needles from rusting and restrains their movements so as to preserve the points.

Stock up with at least half a dozen of each size you want to use. These little devils have a predictable tendency to get lost.

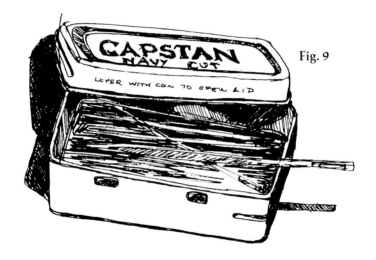

Fig. 9

Palm

The common, Anglo-American style of hand-seaming palm (**Fig. 10,** foreground) consists of a leather sling that is strapped around one's working hand, performing the same function as a seamstress's thimble when entering a needle. The butt of the threaded needle is placed within the circular, raised "iron" section to brace against one of a number of indentations provided for this purpose. A seaming palm may have more than a dozen small, shallow indentations in its iron to take fine needles.

The roping palm with its thumb guard (**Fig. 10,** background), which has been recommended in this book's introduction for its versatility, has only seven, but more substantial, indentations. These do excellently in holding firmly the gamut of needle sizes and, since a roping palm is far hardier than a seaming palm, it is certainly to be preferred.

To prevent injury from an accidental slip of the needle, palms have a raised buttress around the iron, and a pigskin "plate" stitched to the outside of the leather sling. In a first-class palm, the iron's surface will be perpendicular to the natural thrust of the needle to insure as safe an operation as possible.

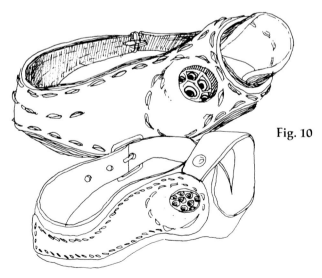

Fig. 10

The best insurance, however, is to hold the needle correctly to begin with. Steer it into one of the indentations in the iron with your ring finger and make sure it remains in place by keeping the fingertip on it. Use the middle fingertip and thumb to direct the needle, and the tip of the index finger as sort of an advance scout, probing the canvas, making directional readjustments to the tip of the needle, or bracing the canvas against the push of the needle. You have to let go this excellent hold every time you take a stitch, of course, but it should be resumed automatically as soon as the needle is pulled through. The exception is when you want to wind the twine around the thumb guard of a roping palm to heave tight on a stitch, in which case the needle is held under the righthand ring finger while the pull is made.

Many of the sailmaker's palms commercially offered today—particularly seaming palms—are not up to the old-time standard, consisting as they do of a flimsy hunk of leather (or even plastic!) with a piece of tin haphazardly sewn on in lieu of a bona fide iron. So when you shop for a palm, look for sturdy leather construction. The leather in a properly-made roping palm will be $\frac{1}{4}''$ thick, and the plate at least half that in addition.

A well-made palm is a prized possession and a pleasure to work with, and ought not to be underrated. The important thing when fitting a palm is that it doesn't pinch at any place, such as around the base of the thumb, but fits snugly and comfortably over the entire hand. If your local ship chandlery can't oblige, it may be worthwhile to write to a reputable manufacturer such as Wm. Smith & Son of Redditch, England, and order a Sailmaker's Roping Palm directly from them.

When you've found your ideal partner, rather than using the watchband buckle usually provided for adjustment as shown in the seaming palm drawing, trim down the ends of the bands so that they don't overlap and chafe your hand, and secure with a neat, seamanlike, permanent seizing as in the roping palm.

The breaking-in of a new palm will take place over a period of time. Simply use it to the extent that your own sweat, or hand moisture if you prefer, softens it up. Eventually it will mold itself, then harden to an exact fit. If you obtain a second-hand palm, or one which is generally a sorry fit, you may want to try soaking the palm for a few hours in lukewarm water to make it more pliable and thus more likely to readjust itself to your hand. I would hesitate to recommend this with a really old palm, however, since the plate may have been secured with animal glue. This will tend to run during a soaking, impairing the homogeneity of the palm as well as discoloring it.

If treated with care and kept in a dry place, a good palm properly broken in will be a joy forever. When I called by to see Everett Lohnes at his Lunenburg, Nova Scotia, sail loft one September day, he pulled out half-a-dozen roping palms which had belonged to sailmakers working a lifetime in that once busy sailing port. One palm had been badly chipped around its iron, but the others all were in perfect order, with smooth pigskin plates gleaming more richly than the autumn sunlight in the harbor. And my own favorite palm was graciously handed on to me long ago by an older colleague at his retirement.

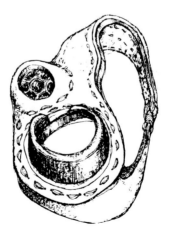

Fig. 11

Beeswax

If you've ever ventured into the glades of Sherwood Forest with Pyle as your guide, you may remember catching a glimpse of Little John in the shade of the greenwood tree, "rolling a stout bow string from long strands of hempen thread . . . and rolling the cord upon his thigh." As he rubbed his new-made string with yellow beeswax to fix the twist, Robin Hood, who had been gazing ruminatively at his chief steward's doings, gave voice to an idea. The adventure that ensues is the one where Little John, in the guise of a holy friar, makes bold to pick up three pretty lasses at the Tuxford crossroads . . . but I have to break off here to point rather to Little John's prowess with the beeswax.

His procedure, of waxing doubled twine, then twisting it, and waxing it again to keep the twist in and stabilize the cordage, is exactly how you should prepare a length of twine for general seaming (for the twine itself, see next entry). The beeswax is a fragrant pale yellow or amber commodity, which you can track down these days at ship chandlers, sailmakers, and (in Europe at least) apothecaries.

Begin by taking a fathom of twine from your spool and threading it through a needle. Double the twine (you now will have a 3' length) and, with a lump of beeswax in your left hand, wax the twine by pulling it hard against the lump (**Fig. 11**).

Then twist the twine, making a counterclockwise turn with your left hand, and a clockwise one with your right (**Fig. 12**). A second and third waxing will keep the twist in and help the twine to flow smoothly through canvas without tangling.

If you require a stopper knot after threading and twisting the twine to prevent the end from working loose as the seaming begins, make a loop as shown in **Fig. 13,** pinch the twine juncture (arrow) between thumb and forefinger, and pull the needle through. It is much better to sew in the end as you go along, however.

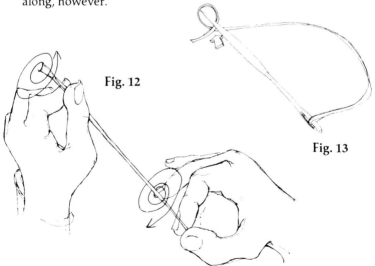

Fig. 12

Fig. 13

Righthand twist, pre-waxed polyester is the flat, pliable twine most commonly used for hand seaming. It is strong and very satisfactory to work with. But for jobs with an ornamental aspect, such as sewn rings, the only real alternative—round-lay polyester—will stand out much more distinctly, both on account of its extra body and because of the more solidly white color.

Twine of the pre-waxed variety supposedly can be used without hand waxing, but if you apply the customary rub-down to it previously discussed, you will find that it holds the twist much better.

If you do a significant amount of hand seaming, buy your twine in a large spool (**Fig. 14**) rather than in some over-priced smaller package.

In addition to multipurpose hand-seaming twine, you will want a spool of fine polyester-and-cotton machine thread. Try to obtain the grade used by sailmakers for light sail or spinnaker seams. The primary use for this fine but strong thread is for whipping wire, where it will give a tight and hard surface after waxing. Since wire whipping is a basic skill, perhaps it is well to introduce it here.

To perform an elementary wire whipping—in this case as applied to wire strands prefatory to splicing—take a length of hand-waxed machine thread and put the standing part (the locked end of the twine, as distinguished from the free or "working" end) along the strand and make a series of clockwise turns, as shown in **Fig. 15.** The whipping is then finished off with at least two half hitches before the ends are cut flush.

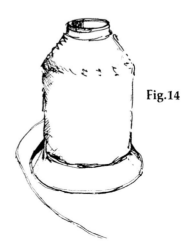

Fig.14

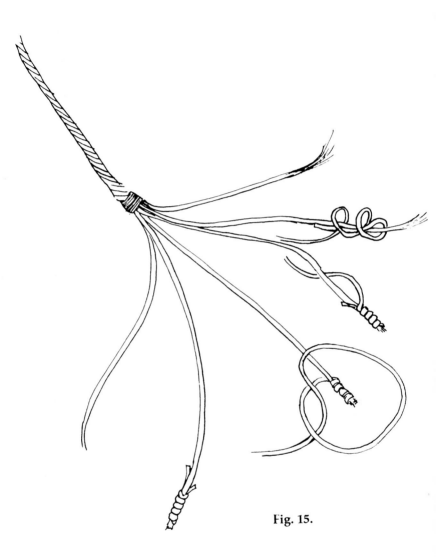

Fig. 15.

Sailmaker's Hook

As mentioned earlier, a canvas-piercing hook is indispensable in that it provides an "extra hand" in any kind of hand-seaming work.

The most commonly used model consists of a 3″ piece of round steel which has a bronze swivel at one end for a spliced-in lanyard, and a pointed hook at the other for insertion in the canvas (**Fig. 16**).

However, the point commercially supplied serves very poorly in this context, since it is on the blunt side and difficult to press into the canvas. If really drawn to a firm hold, it leaves a gaping hole or, quite possibly, a rip.

To prevent such mishaps, you must sharpen the ends of these hooks with a file as shown in the sketch (dotted line represents the original shape of the point). The sharp end then allows the hook to enter canvas smoothly, while the bulge prevents it from entering so far as to make a big hole or rip.

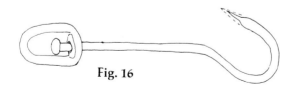

Fig. 16

Prickers, Spikes and Fids

Spikes of iron, whale bone, or hardwood were among the earliest canvas- and rope-working tools. They were used to pierce canvas for sewing and to pry apart the strands of a rope for splicing. In time, these primitive tools were developed into highly specialized instruments.

Piercing tools known as prickers (round or square section) and stabbers (with the superior three-square section) have become sharp and effective but, for the purpose of the ditty bag, rather cumbersome to carry. An obvious substitute is our friend, the sharp knife. Pierce a star-shaped hole by taking three strokes to the center, pry it open with a fid, and cut off the tatters with the knife.

If you need to make a lot of holes, by far the best instrument is a regular hole punch which cuts a neat, circular hole (see *Spur Teeth Grommet* section).

For piercing small holes—to make way for the needle in repairing boating mocassins, for example (but even then, sewing through the rubber sole is murderous)—I find an awl of the kind used in leather work the handiest tool (**Fig. 17**). The sharp end of this tool, as with any such pointed implement, should be protected with a cork.

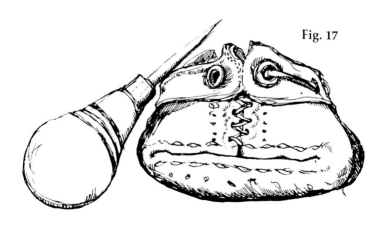

Fig. 17

The classic, hand-forged cast steel marlinspike (**Fig. 18**) used mostly for splicing wire often comes in a length of ten inches or so, and is evenly tapered down from about an inch diameter at its base. Riggers of my acquaintance sometimes prefer an oval section further flattened at the working end so that it enters easily between strands and then can be twisted so as to make as large a passage as possible for the strand to be tucked through.

With any splicing tool, the technique for entering between strands is the same. The spike or fid is held in the right hand and positioned along the lay of the rope or wire. While the left hand supports the rope, the left thumb forces the tip of the fid into the score (**Fig. 19**). The tool is levered into a

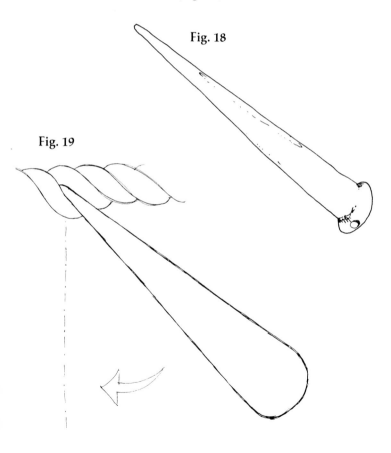

Fig. 18

Fig. 19

perpendicular position (arrow) and pressed between the strands. With a bit of practice, you should be able to coordinate this sequence into one swift motion.

The traditional marlinspike, however, has little function among the narrow wire gauges involved in most yachts' running and standing rigging. Its successor in this area in all but name is the hollow-coned Swedish fid (**Fig. 20**). An excellent ditty bag utensil, especially in the handy 7″ length, this tool carries a misnomer. "Fid" denotes a rope-working tool, but the Swedish fid is as much a wire splicer's companion. The advantage of the hollow stainless steel cone is that you can enter and then leave it in position, passing a strand through the hollow at leisure. With a regular marlinspike or fid, you have to overcompensate when entering, then quickly withdraw the spike and hope that a strand can be passed through before the rapidly contracting opening has become too small. Swedish fids will benefit from a flattening of the tip with a file for ease of entry.

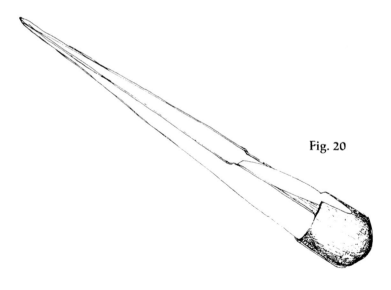

Fig. 20

Rope-working fids of the first order are made from lignum vitae or pockenholz. The former is a light-colored hardwood from the tropical guaiacum tree, and is strong and fairly smooth in its grain. But as a fid material, it takes second place to pockenholz, a very heavy, dark hardwood with a natural oil in the fibers which makes the surface incomparably smooth and silky. The color is almost pitch black in the sought-after form, with streaks of nutty brown away from the center.

Fids made from plain oak are more readily available and should be soaked repeatedly in linseed oil to maintain a hard, smooth surface.

Fig. 21 depicts a fid size well suited to the ditty bag and general on-board splicing work. The turk's head knot enhances the grip somewhat, but is mainly decorative.

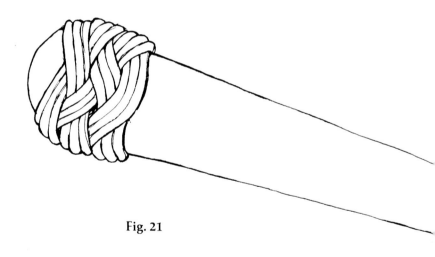

Fig. 21